Tiny Tinkles Little Music

Wiggle Wiggle
Jiggle Jiggle
Fingerplays with Friends

Created by **Debra Krol** Pictures by **Corinne Orazietti & Melanie Hawkins**

This book is dedicated to
all the little people for inspiring me,
and all the BIG people for believing in me.

Copyright © 2021 Tiny Tinkles Publishing Company

All Rights Reserved.

No parts of this publication or the characters in it, may be reproduced or distributed in any form or by any means without written permission from the publisher.

To request permission, or for school visits and book readings, please visit www.tinytinkles.com

ISBN (Paperback): 978-1-7777050-9-1

ISBN (Ebook): 978-1-990563-00-3

First Edition 2021
Author/Creator: Debra Krol
Pictures by: Corinne Orazietti & Melanie Hawkins
Editor: Tanya Guenther

HOW TO READ THIS BOOK

Read the story. Have fun! Use silly voices and make animal sounds.

Talk about what you see. Each of the **WIGGLE FRIENDS** in this book represent FINGERS on your hands. The fingers are the same for each hand and have corresponding finger numbers. Place your hands together, like you are clapping your hands. Start counting from ONE with your THUMB, all the way to your PINKY 1, 2, 3, 4, 5. Each page of this book has the characters scattered in different orders, allowing you many opportunities to create connections with each character and finger play your way throughout the book. After enjoying the story a few times, take time finding each Wiggle Friend on the page. Your little one will love discovering the new finger patterns on each spread… and feel free to REPEAT!

Tiny Tinkles Little Musician books are designed to grow with your child. Pages and concepts in this book can be used independently or read from cover to cover in one sitting. Introduce learning and concepts as your child is ready.

Wiggle Wiggle Jiggle Jiggle Theme Song
Sing along at www.tinytinkles.com

	Chorus	Wiggle Wiggle, Jiggle Jiggle, dancing all around. Wiggle Wiggle, Jiggle Jiggle, dancing all day long.
	Verse 1	Tommy Thumb is number one, meow meow number one. Tommy Thumb is number one, meow meow number one.
	Verse 2	Parker Penguin is number two, doot doot number two. Parker Penguin is number two, doot doot number two.
	Verse 3	Missy Mouse is number three, squeak squeak number three. Missy Mouse is number three, squeak squeak number three.
	Verse 4	Rosie Rabbit is number four, hop hop number four. Rosie Rabbit is number four, hop hop number four.
	Verse 5	Pokey Porcupine is number five, poke poke number five. Pokey Porcupine is number five, poke poke number five.

Videos, worksheets, and more resources at www.tinytinkles.com

It's a lovely day in **Tiny Tinkles Town.**

The birds are singing and the sun is smiling bright. It's the perfect day to wiggle, jiggle, and make beautiful **music** together.

Let's wave and say HELLO to the Wiggle Friends.

Tommy Thumb stomps his paws, and meows out to his friends...

one
two
ready
GO!

The **Wiggle Friends** are all warmed up! Now it's time to sing, wiggle and jiggle to their groovy song at the **Dance Party.**

The friends wait patiently for the music to start...

Wiggle wiggle, jiggle jiggle, dancing all around.
Wiggle wiggle, jiggle jiggle, dancing all day long.

Tommy Thumb is number 1... **MEOW MEOW** number one.

Tommy Thumb is number 1, **MEOW MEOW** number 1.

Parker Penguin is number 2, **DOOT DOOT** number 2.

Parker Penguin is number 2, **DOOT DOOT** number 2.

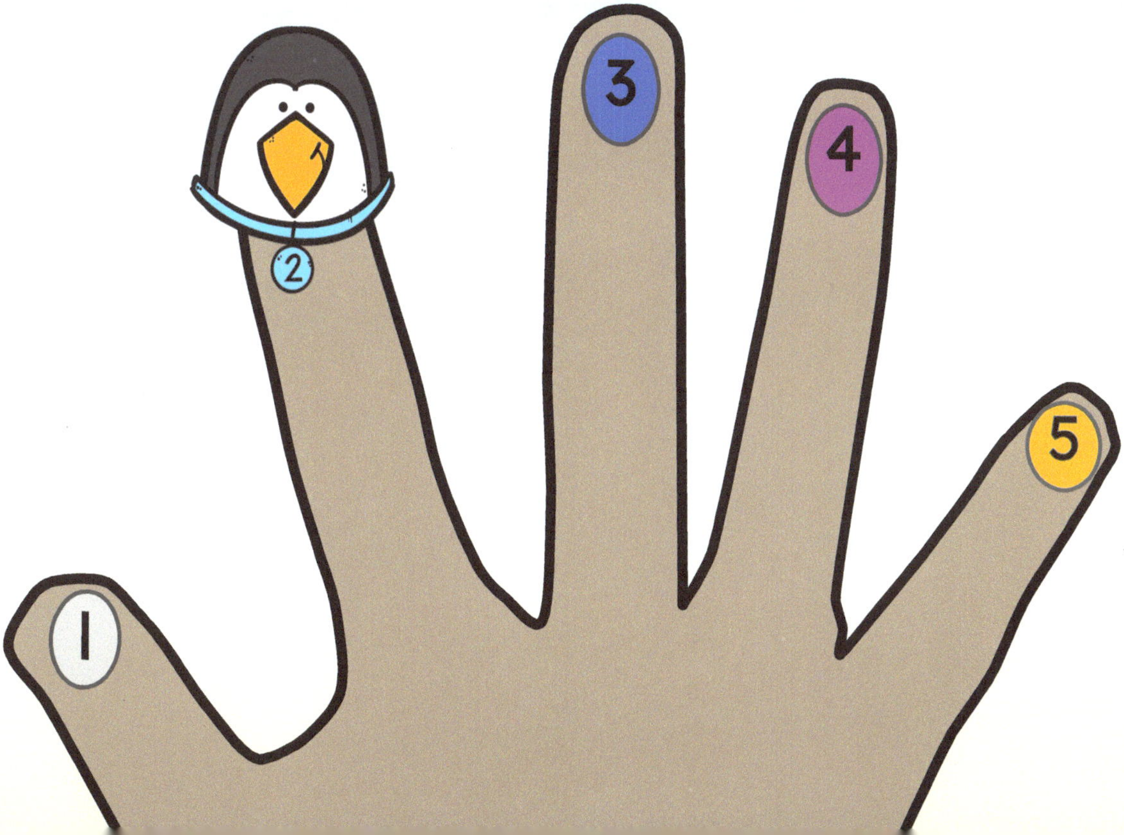

Look...

it's Missy Mouse!

Missy Mouse is number 3, **SQUEAK SQUEAK** number 3.

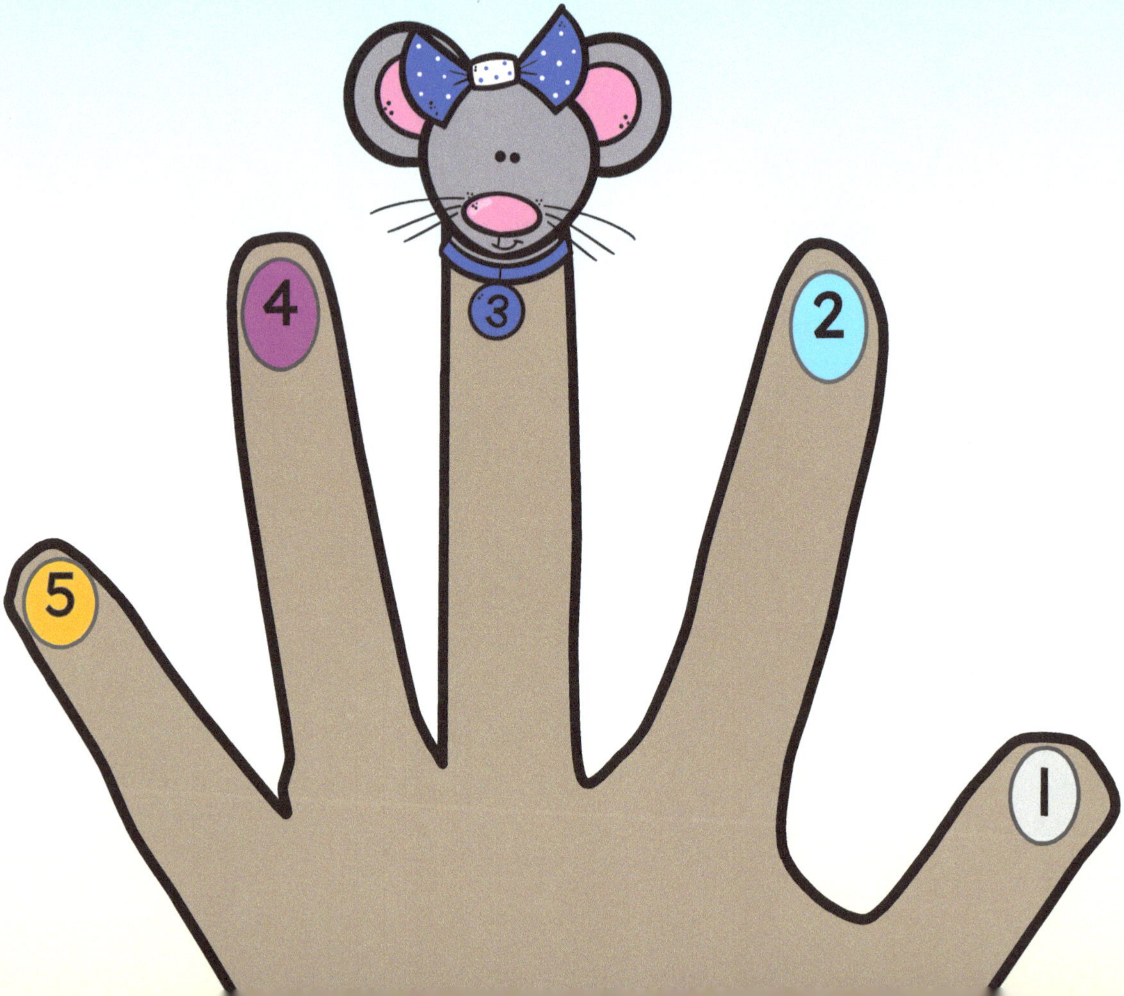

Missy Mouse is number 3, **SQUEAK SQUEAK** number 3.

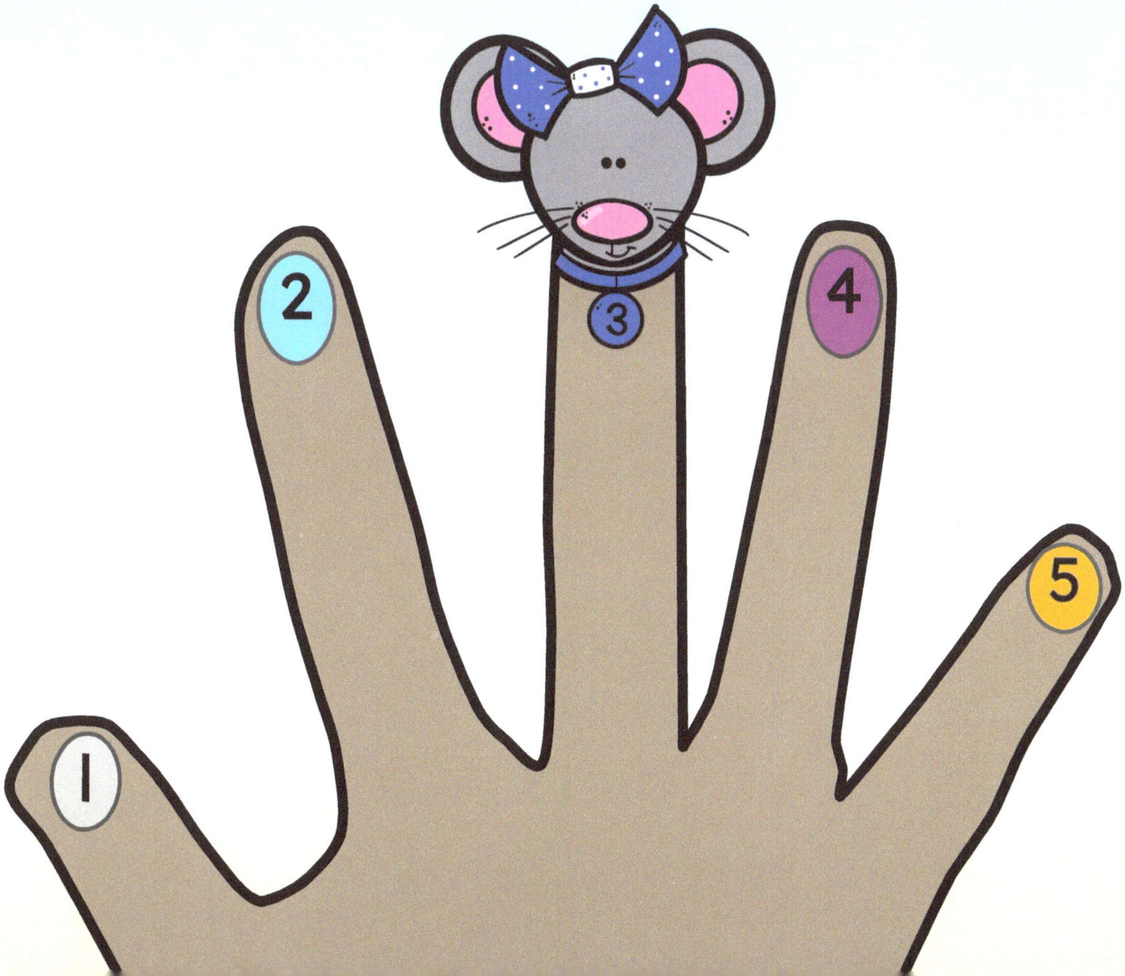

Look...

it's Rosie Rabbit!

Rosie Rabbit is number 4, **HOP HOP** number 4.

Rosie Rabbit is number 4, **HOP HOP** number 4.

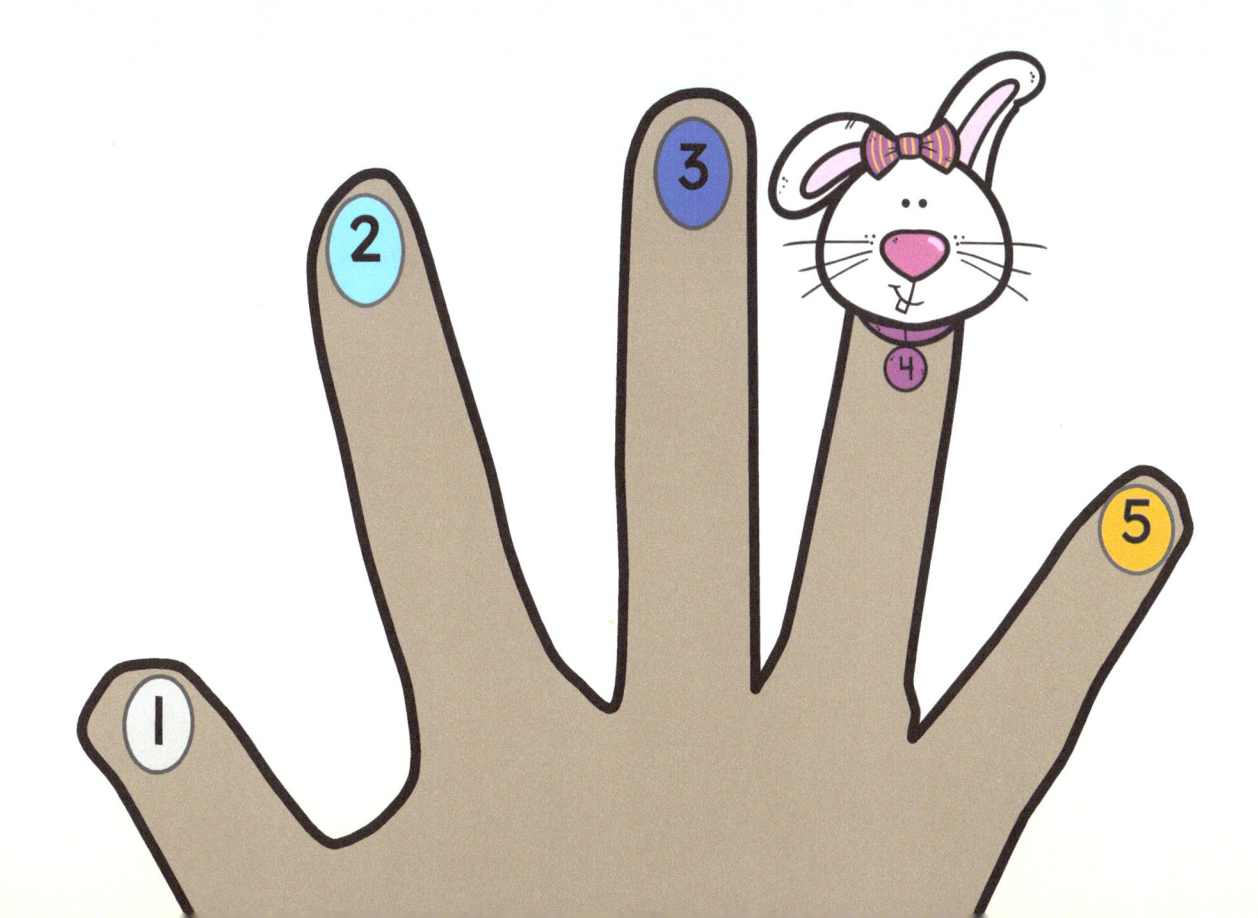

Wiggle wiggle, jiggle jiggle,
dancing all around.
Wiggle wiggle, jiggle jiggle,
dancing all day long.

Look...
it's Pokey Porcupine!

Pokey Porcupine is number 5, **POKE POKE** number 5.

Pokey Porcupine is number 5, **POKE POKE** number 5.

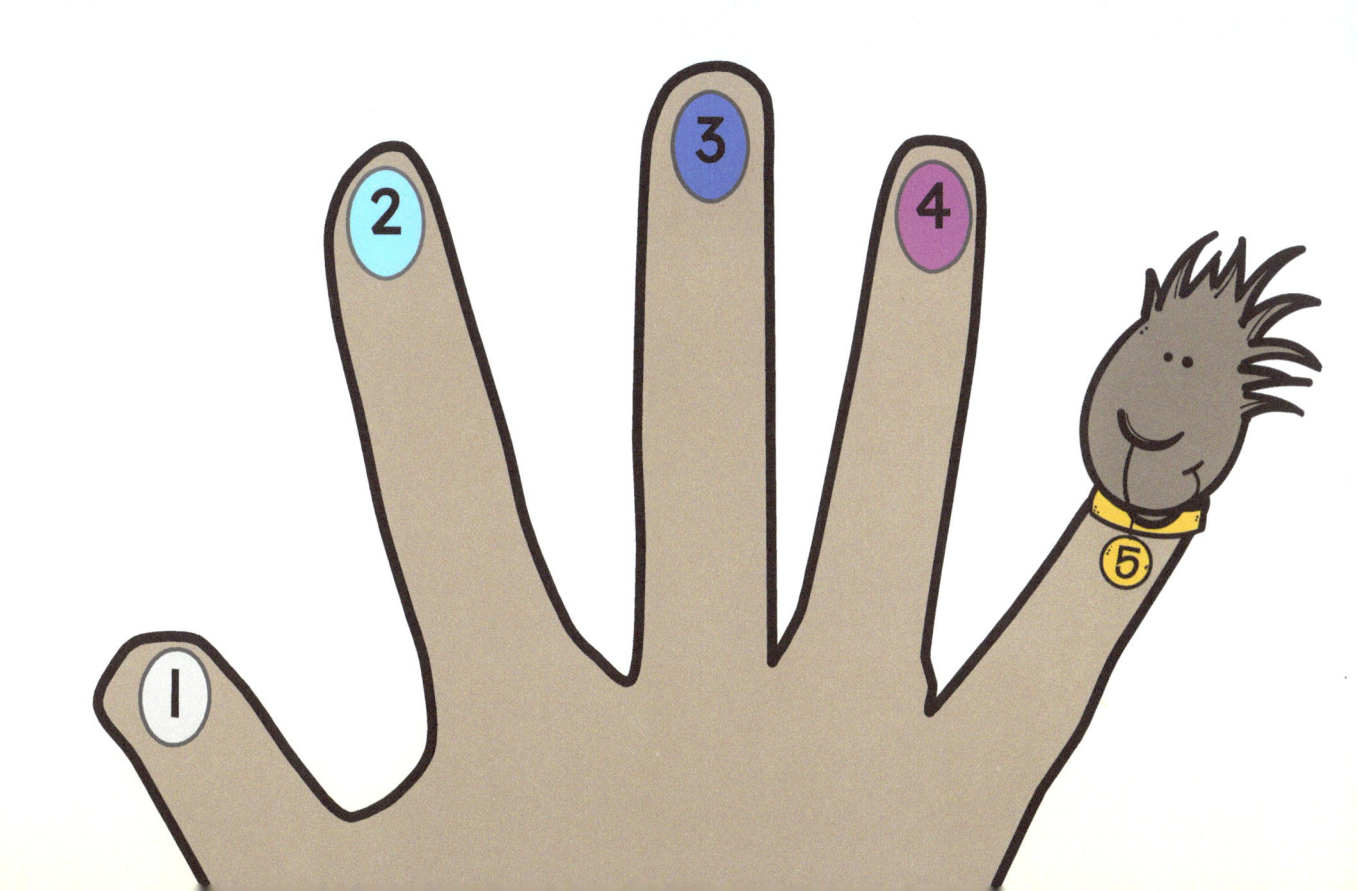

As the dance party ends, the Wiggle Friends agree...
dancing is fun!
Mr. Repeat cheers, "let's do it all AGAIN!"

REPEAT!

Fine... the End.

POP! the Bubble GAME

Draw the activity cards to find the friends and pop their bubbles with the correct finger.

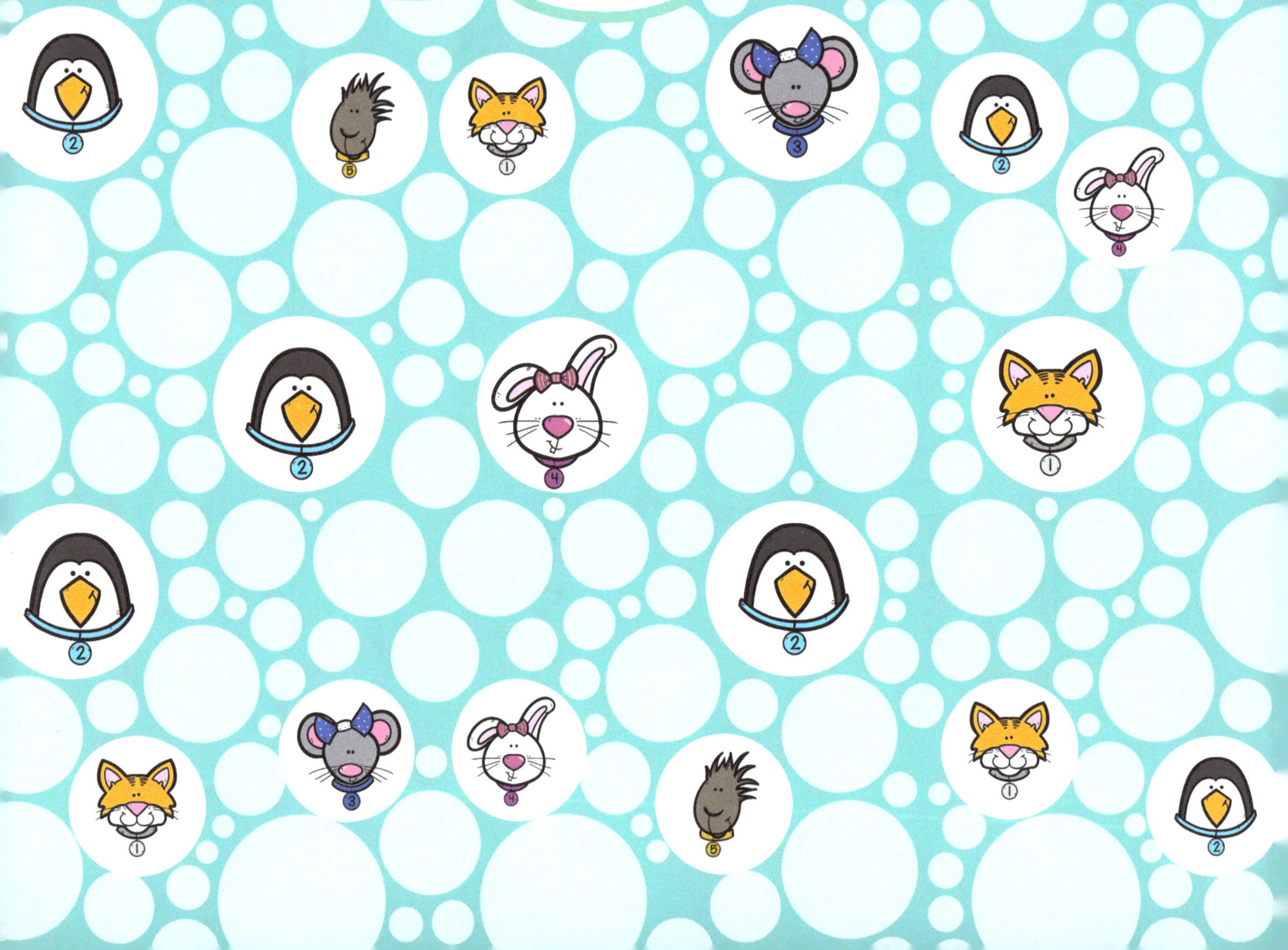

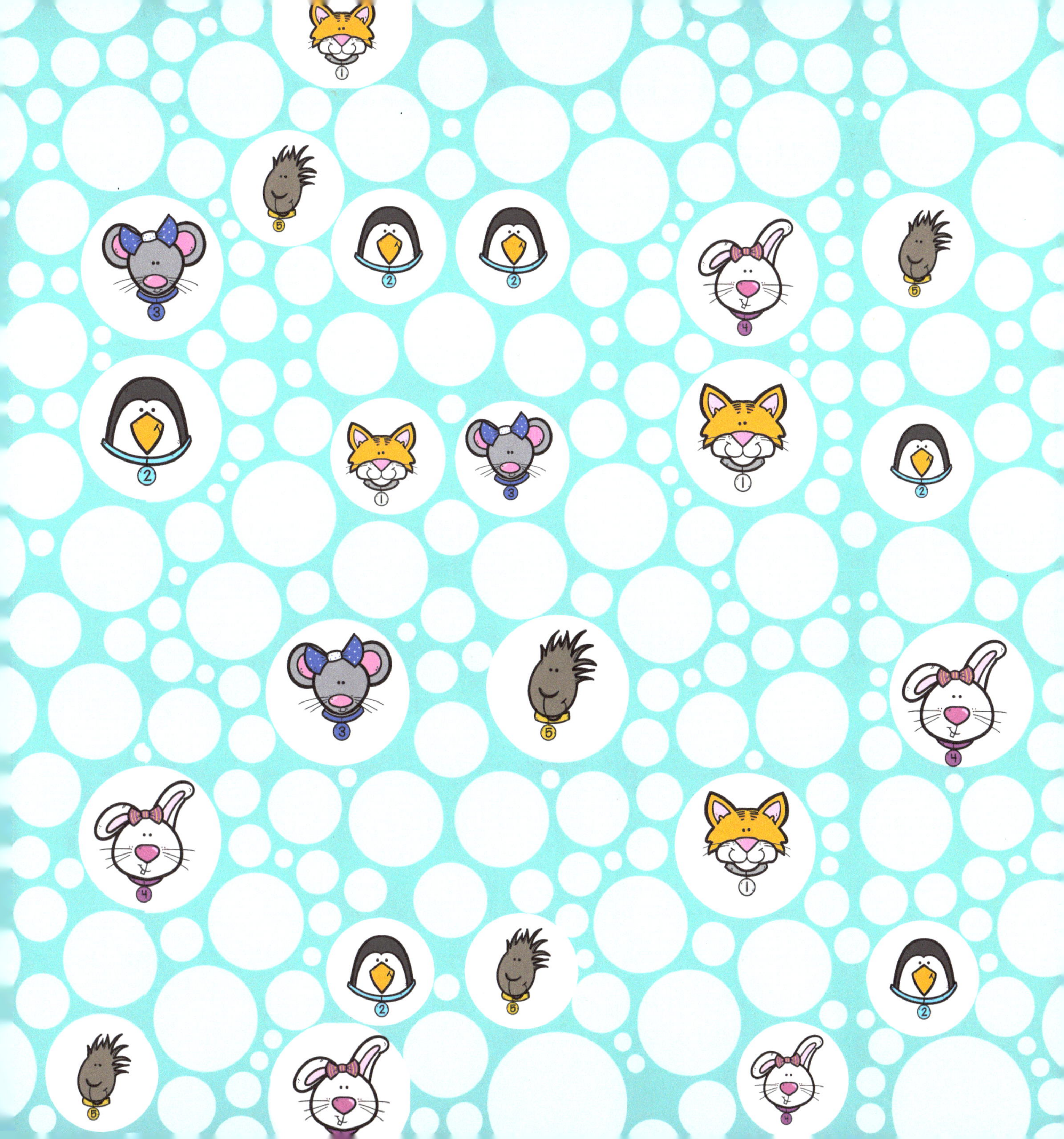

INSTRUCTIONS for Activity Cards

- **FIND** each Wiggle Friend on your hand to match the Animal cards.

- **MATCH** the Wiggle Friend card with the correct fingers and the correct numbers with all cards facing up.

- **FIND** each finger on your hand to match the Hand Print cards.

- **MATCH** the Number Cards with the Wiggle Friends.

- **PLAY** a game of memory with all of the cards, they just need to match in some sort of form to be a pair. Tommy Thumb matches the number 1 and also the thumb, you could also match the hands together to identify the same fingers.

- **POP** Shuffle the cards. Place five cards in a row. Using the correct finger number as pictured in the cards, POP the cards with the correct finger just like you pop the bubbles!

BONUS! Wiggle Friend Rings

No need to laminate! Adjust the rings on your child's fingers and use tape to secure. Kids LOVE to wear the rings during storytime. The rings are very helpful for easily finding each Wiggle Friend.

1 2 3 4 5

1 2 3 4 5

ABOUT THE CREATORS

Debra Krol is a BC Registered Music Teacher who specializes in teaching music to babies, toddlers and preschoolers. She is also a children's songwriter and author. Ms. Deb enjoys camping with her hubby, kids, and Daisy Dog, their black and tan coonhound. She loves playing piano, ukulele, guitar and most of all, singing & drawing with all of her little friends!

▶ Tiny Tinkles Music Studio   f tinytinkles

Corinne Orazietti was a preschool and elementary teacher for many years. She saw how her whimsical illustrations added sparkle to her lessons and decided it was time to share her passion for art with others. She now works as a full-time artist at her company, Chirp Graphics, and spends her days drawing cartoon dragons and fairies.

◯ chirpgraphics   f chirpgraphicsclipart

Melanie Hawkins is an author, illustrator, elementary art teacher and mom to seven children! Her family is her greatest source of joy and inspiration. She enjoys camping, swimming, dark chocolate, and movie nights with her family. Melanie is an eternal optimist and wishes that everyone could see the world as she does with all of its beauty, hope and goodness.

🌐 melaniehawkinsauthor.com   ◯ inspirejoypublishing

We are GROWING! More books in the series available soon!

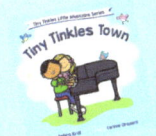

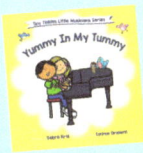

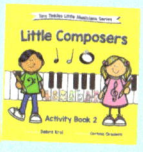

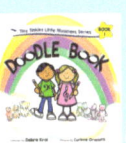

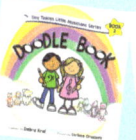

CPSIA information can be obtained
at www.ICGtesting.com
Printed in the USA
LVHW072102140422
716231LV00002B/33